MAGIC
Step-by-Step

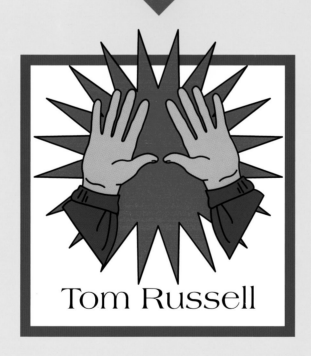

Tom Russell

Sterling Publishing Co., Inc.   New York
A Sterling/Chapelle Book

This book is dedicated to my nephew,
Jesse H. Gamez Iacovetto,
whose magical personality and magic tricks
bring joy to all those who love him.

For Chapelle
Owner: Jo Packham
Editor: Cathy Sexton
Computer Diagrams: Amber Hansen
Magician Consultant: Steve Bauter
Staff: Malissa Boatwright, Kass Burchett, Rebecca Christensen,
Marilyn Goff, Shirley Heslop, Holly Hollingsworth, Susan Jorgensen,
Susan Laws, Barbara Milburn, Pat Pearson, Leslie Ridenour,
Cindy Rooks, and Cindy Stoeckl

If you have any questions or comments or would like information on specialty
products featured in this book, please contact Chapelle, Ltd., Inc., P.O. Box 9252,
Ogden, UT 84409 • (801) 621-2777 • (801) 621-2788 Fax

Library of Congress Cataloging-in-Publication Data
Russell, Tom, 1962–
        Magic, step-by-step / Tom Russell.
                p.   cm.
        "A Sterling / Chapelle book."
        Includes index.
        ISBN 0-8069-9533-5
        1. Conjuring. I. Title.
GV1547.R926 1997
793.8—dc20   96-30193
                                                              CIP

10 9 8 7 6 5 4 3 2 1

Published by Sterling Publishing Company, Inc.
387 Park Avenue South, New York, NY 10016
© 1997 by Chapelle Ltd.
Distributed in Canada by Sterling Publishing
c/o Canadian Manda Group, One Atlantic Avenue, Suite 105
Toronto, Ontario, Canada M6K 3E7
Distributed in Great Britain and Europe by Cassell PLC
Wellington House, 125 Strand, London WC2R 0BB, England
Distributed in Australia by Capricorn Link (Australia) Pty Ltd.
P.O. Box 6651, Baulkham Hills, Business Centre, NSW 2153, Australia
Printed and Bound in Hong Kong
All Rights Reserved

Sterling ISBN 0-8069-9533-5

Welcome

When I was a child, my mother told me that if I could play the piano I would be the "hit of every party." I practiced every day and could finally play two tunes.

While I was learning the piano, my brother was wasting his time learning to perform magic tricks.

I guess he didn't realize that I was going to be the hit of every party. What I didn't realize is that every party doesn't have a piano!

So my brother, with his pocket full of tricks stole my audience.

Whether you love being the center of attention or you're shy and would like to develop some self-confidence, this is the book for you! It's your introduction to the world of entertainment.

All you need is to develop a little manual dexterity, some magician's chatter, and a desire to amaze and mystify. Best of all, you don't have to buy expensive props; all of these tricks can be performed with items you find around the house.

First, go into the kitchen and get a lion and a trapeze and then look in the garage for a pretty girl wearing a leotard. Have you got them? Good, let's begin!

Contents

Presentation

Being a magician means believing in yourself. Never do a trick unless you are sold on it. It is frightening enough to get up in front of an audience without adding the further burden of doubting your material. When selecting tricks from this book, look for ones that are compatible with your personality and skill level.

When putting these tricks to the test, even if your knees are knocking, your hands are clammy, and your heart is pounding with fright — try to look as if you are enjoying yourself. An atmosphere of fun and confidence is essential to the effective performance of any magic trick.

There are three simple keys to becoming a good magician: practice, practice, practice! Skill can only come from confidence and, as they say, "practice makes perfect."

Becoming a magician means becoming a master of misdirection. Every aspect of your act is designed to lead your audience somewhere else. These tricks have been designed to inform, intrigue, and rob your audience of concentration. While your hands perform the trick, your eyes, voice, and body suggest that the audience should be following your every movement, especially those not involved in the actual performance of the trick!

A good magician has to become a good storyteller, describing the trick while it is being performed. Try to use words and phrases that you feel comfortable with. And, remember the importance of misdirecting the watchful eye.

If you are working a small audience, try to involve them. Let them make choices, answer questions, and feel that they are a part of the trick. Participants will be more amazed when the trick is completed knowing they were a part of it, and they still don't know how it was done.

There are illusionists and magicians. An illusionist relies upon stage setting, dramatic theatrics, and a gullible audience. A magician relies upon tricks that can be performed up close, allowing the audience to almost be a part of the trick.

There are two kinds of people in any magician's audience. Those who want to enjoy the trick and be amazed and those who want to discover how the trick is done and discredit the magician.

This leads us to the most important rules of magic:

◆ One, never repeat a trick, no matter how much your audience pleads.

continued ...

Good magic is like eating a box of chocolates. One or two pieces will make anyone happy — a whole box in one sitting will always make you sick! The trick is to keep your audience wanting more.

◆ Two, *never, never* reveal how a trick is done! This is the most important rule of magic.

Whether you are performing for a room full of spectators or for one person in the checkout line at your local grocery store, always perform to the portion of your audience that wants to be amazed. That amazement can only come from being unable to figure out how you did it. The truth is, they really don't want to know. We all want to believe in magic and your job is to ensure that we do.

Learn these tricks, become a master of misdirection, and be faithful to the magician's creed and you will develop a skill that will serve you well.

And, always remember ... a pocketful of tricks is easier to carry than a piano!

Disappearing Acts

"Magic
should
not be
just magic,
it should
also be
entertaining."

Disintegrating Thimble

Materials Needed: One thimble.
Object of Trick: To make the thimble disappear.

STEP 1
Call in your audience and seat them in front of you, keeping them there at all times. Next, place the thimble on your right index finger.

STEP 2
Bend your finger so the thimble is secure between your thumb and your index finger.

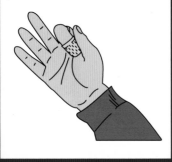

STEP 3
Slowly straighten your index finger, leaving the thimble resting where it was placed, and carefully hold all your fingers apart. The thimble will appear to have disintegrated.

Bend your index finger down again and pick up the thimble. Do this quickly so the thimble will reappear!

Throw-Away Thimble

Materials Needed: One thimble.

Object of Trick: To make the thimble disappear.

STEP 1
Call in your aud-ience and seat them in front of you, keeping them there at all times. Next, place the thimble in your right hand.

STEP 2
Make a throwing motion upward as if you were actually throw-ing the thimble into the air.

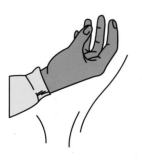

STEP 3
As your audience is looking for the thimble, bend your fing-er so the thimble is secure between your thumb and your index finger.

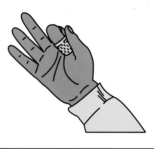

STEP 4
If you choose to have the thim-ble reappear, quickly reach behind your el-bow, behind your ear, under the table, or into your pocket to retrieve the thimble!

Vanishing Salt Shaker

Materials Needed: One dime, one cloth napkin, and one salt shaker.

Object of Trick: To make the salt shaker disappear.

STEP 1

Call in your audience and seat them in front of you, keeping them there at all times. Next, place the dime on the table in front of you. Tightly cover the salt shaker with the napkin. Make certain the napkin clings to the salt shaker and takes on its shape.

STEP 2

Pick up the salt shaker and slowly begin rubbing it in a circular motion over the dime.

STEP 3

At the same time, quickly move the covered salt shaker toward you, almost to the table's edge, and slap your other hand over the dime before anyone can see if it's there or not.

"Table magic is fun because your audience doesn't understand that the table helps you."

STEP 4
Slowly lift your hand to reveal that the dime is still there.

STEP 5
Pick up the salt shaker and once again slowly begin rubbing it over the dime.

STEP 6
This time, as you quickly move the salt shaker toward you and slap your other hand over the dime, make certain the salt shaker is moved toward you close enough to drop into your lap.

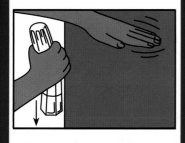

STEP 7
The napkin, still in the shape of the salt shaker, should be set down away from the dime. Once again, slowly lift your hand to reveal that the dime is *still* there.

STEP 8
As you express your anger, slap your hand over the covered salt shaker. Because the salt shaker has been dropped into your lap, it will appear that it vanished!

Oh, Sugar! Where Are You?

Materials Needed: One wrapped sugar cube.
Object of Trick: To make the sugar cube disappear.

STEP 1
Prepare this trick by unwrapping the sugar cube and re-moving it from its wrapper. Once the sugar cube has been re-moved, fold the wrapper back up so it appears that the sugar cube is still inside.

STEP 2
Call in your aud-ience and seat them in front of you. Next, place the sugar cube wrapper on the table in front of you and move it around. Place the sugar cube in your lap.

STEP 3
Raise your right hand over the sugar cube wrapper and slap it down so you have flattened the wrapper. It will appear that the sugar cube has vanished!

STEP 4
You can take this trick one step further by reaching under the table with your left hand as though to "catch" the sugar cube as it is forced to pene-trate the surface of the table!

Rub-A-Dub-Dub

Materials Needed: One dime.

Object of Trick: To make the dime disappear.

STEP 1
Call in your audience and seat them in front of you, keeping them there at all times. Next, show the dime to your audience.

STEP 3
After rubbing for a few minutes, accidentally drop the dime onto the floor. As you bend down to pick it up, quickly drop it into your shoe.

STEP 2
Place the dime on the back of your left hand and, with your right hand, slowly begin rubbing it up and down.

STEP 4
Continue bringing your hand up as if you have the dime. Assume your position of rubbing the dime slowly on the back of your left hand. After a few more minutes, announce that the dime has finally been rubbed away!

Disappearing Dime

Materials Needed: One dime, one white handkerchief, and one white bar of soap.

Object of Trick: To make the dime disappear.

STEP 1

Prepare this trick by cutting a sliver from the bar of soap and mashing it onto one corner of the handkerchief. The soap must be invisible, therefore you must use a white handkerchief and a white bar of soap.

STEP 2

Call in your audience and seat them in front of you, keeping them there at all times. Next, spread the handkerchief out on the table in front of you and place the dime in the center.

STEP 3

One corner at a time, fold the four corners of the handkerchief toward the center onto the dime. Make certain you begin with the soaped corner.

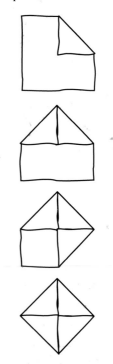

STEP 4

Ask someone from your audience to make sure the dime is still in the handkerchief. He (she) should do this by pressing on the dime. The pressure will stick the dime to the soaped corner.

STEP 6

The dime should be stuck to one of the top corners of the handkerchief and should slide right into your hand.

Hidden dime

STEP 5

Place your hands back to back and insert your fingers into the crease nearest you.

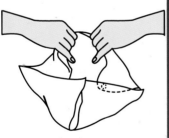

Keep your eye on the corner that has the dime. At the same time, quickly lift and spread the handkerchief open into a vertically displayed position.

STEP 7

Hold the handkerchief up at the edge of the table and drop the dime into your lap. Show your audience both sides of the handkerchief and show them that both of your hands are empty!

Evanescent Quarter

Materials Needed: One quarter.

Object of Trick: To make the quarter disappear.

STEP 1

Prepare this trick by making up an incredible story — maybe about how coins are made or how the chemistry of the human body can degrade the luster of the metallic elements that make up a quarter.

STEP 2

Call in your audience and seat them in front of you, keeping them there at all times. Next, pick up the quarter with your right hand and show it to your audience.

STEP 3

Place the quarter in your left hand and prop your chin on your right hand. Begin rubbing the quarter on your right forearm. Make certain you hold the quarter so it is not visible. Then, as you continue rubbing the quarter on your forearm, begin telling the story that you have painstakingly made up!

Quarter

STEP 4

Next, you should allow the quarter to slip out of your left hand and drop onto the table. All the while you should be continuing with your story and should have eye contact with your audience.

STEP 5

To pick up the dropped quarter, use the hand that has been propping your chin. Pretend to pass the quarter from your right hand back into your left hand. Once again, prop your chin in the palm of your right hand and continue rubbing the quarter. The fake pass must be done very carefully and make certain that your story has not been interrupted.

STEP 6

Rub a little longer. Break your eye contact with your audience and look as though something has gone terribly wrong. Rub a little harder and begin smiling.

STEP 7

Start to slow down the rubbing and slowly begin lifting your fingers, one at a time. As you do this, carefully drop the quarter into your shirt at the neckline. Show your audience that both of your hands are empty!

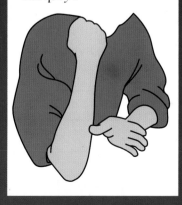

19

Dissolving Quarter

Materials Needed: One quarter, one small straight-sided glass, and one handkerchief.

Object of Trick: To make the quarter disappear.

STEP 1
Prepare this trick by filling the glass half full with water.

STEP 2
Call in your audience and seat them in front of you, keeping them there at all times. Next, drape the handkerchief over the palm of your right hand. Place the quarter in the center of the handkerchief and pinch it through the cloth with your thumb and index finger.

STEP 3
Turn your right hand over, allowing the handkerchief to hang down.

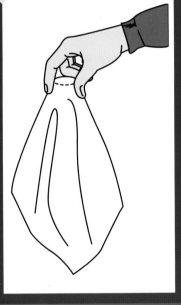

"The more you practice, the better you will get."

STEP 4

Pick up the glass of water and hold it underneath the handkerchief. Once the glass is hidden by the handkerchief, tilt the glass toward you. Once the glass is in the correct position, drop the quarter into the handkerchief so it hits the outside of the glass. You must catch the quarter in your fingertips.

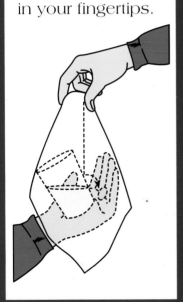

STEP 5

The sound of the quarter hitting the outside of the glass will fool your audience into believing the quarter has fallen into the glass of water. Allow the handkerchief to settle over the rim of the glass while you let the quarter fall from your fingertips into the palm of your hand. Adjust the glass in your left hand so it covers the quarter.

Quarter

STEP 6

Carefully remove the handkerchief and allow your audience to look down into the glass of water. The quarter will be visible through the bottom of the glass and will look like it is in the water.

STEP 7

Using the handkerchief, re-cover the glass. Ask someone from your audience to remove the glass from your hand and place it on the table in front of you. As the glass is removed, close your hand, concealing the quarter. Move your hand toward you close enough to drop the quarter into your lap. Quickly move your left hand back toward the glass and point at it.

STEP 8

Have the assistant from your audience remove the handkerchief from the glass on the table. The coin will be gone. Show your audience both sides of the handkerchief and show them that both of your hands are empty!

"Always practice in front of a mirror so you can see what your audience sees."

Cards & Coins

"Magic
at its
finest
requires
two things:
practice
and belief."

One-Way Card

Materials Needed: One deck of playing cards.

Object of Trick: To choose which face card has been picked up and turned around.

STEP 1

Prepare this trick by studying the faces on the face cards. The bottom half of the cards will appear to be exactly the same as the top half. However, if you look hard enough, you will be able to detect slight differences. Each deck of playing cards will vary and the imperfections might be incredibly slight. If you cannot see any apparent differences, you might need to concentrate on a certain shape in the design, such as a "heart" on the king's robe.

STEP 2

Call in your audience and seat them in front of you. Next, remove four face cards from the deck and place them in a row on the table. As you place them down, look at them carefully to detect which cards you have chosen and to observe the direction they face.

STEP 3

Turn around and ask someone from your audience to turn one of the cards 180°. Turn back around; study them and pick the one that was rotated!

Spelling Bee

Materials Needed: One deck of playing cards.

Object of Trick: To be able to spell out the card numbers and then turn over the matching card.

STEP 1

Prepare this trick by removing the following cards, *in any suit,* from the deck: one of each number from ace through king — ace, 2, 3, 4, 5, 6, 7, 8, 9, 10, jack, queen, and king. Next, arrange the cards in the following order: 3 (on top), 8, 7, ace, queen, 6, 4, 2, jack, king, 10, 9, and 5 (on bottom). Return them to the top of the deck.

STEP 2

Call in your audience and seat them in front of you. Shuffle the cards, but do not disturb the top 13 cards.

STEP 3

Next, count and remove the 13 cards from the top of the deck. Set the rest of the deck aside.

STEP 4

Place the cards, face down, in your left hand. Spell the name of each card, as you move one card from the top of the pile to the bottom for each letter. Spell A-C-E. When ACE is complete, the next card will be an ace! Place the ace on the bottom of the pile and continue on. Next, spell T-W-O, and repeat the process!

A-Drop-in-the-Hat

Materials Needed: One hat and one deck of playing cards.

Object of Trick: To drop the cards into the hat from a height of four feet.

STEP 1

Ask someone from your audience to be your assistant and give him (her) half the deck of cards.

STEP 2

Place the hat, top side down, on the floor in front of you. Remove one card from the deck and hold it about four feet above the floor and over the center of the hat. Tell your audience that you bet you can drop more cards into the hat than your assistant can.

STEP 3

Begin by having your assistant go first. Take one of the cards and, holding it by the end, demonstrate how the cards should be dropped into the hat. One by one, have your assistant attempt to drop the cards into the hat.

STEP 4

The majority of the cards will miss the hat and fall in many directions. When all of your assistant's cards have been dropped, take out the cards that have fallen into the hat and count them. Pick up the cards that were dropped, but did not go into the hat. Make certain you make a big deal about how few, if any, he (she) actually made fall into the hat.

STEP 5

Now it's your turn to show your audience that you can win the bet. Hold the cards flat between your fingers and your thumb, facing the floor.

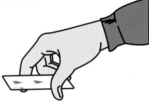

STEP 6

As you drop each card, the cards will fall straight down. If you are standing so you can drop the cards over the center of the hat, you should be able to make nine out of 10 cards fall directly into the hat!

"Magic is performing and acting."

Ace Through Nine

Materials Needed: One deck of playing cards.

Object of Trick: To choose which card, by number, has been removed without looking.

STEP 1

Hand someone from your audience nine cards, *in any suit,* from the deck: one of each number from ace through nine — ace, 2, 3, 4, 5, 6, 7, 8, and 9.

STEP 2

Next, have him (her) shuffle the nine cards as many times as he (she) chooses. While your assistant is shuffling the cards, you should take a seat with your back to the table.

STEP 3

When the cards have been shuffled to his (her) satisfaction, tell him (her) to deal the cards into three rows of three cards each.

STEP 4

Next, have him (her) pick up any one of the cards. He (she) should show the card to the audience and then put it into his (her) pocket.

STEP 5

Now have him (her) add the cards as if doing simple addition. The space where the missing card went should be counted as zero.

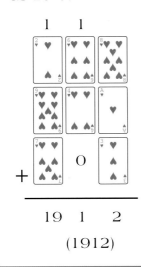

$$1 \quad 1$$

$$+ \quad 0$$

$$19 \quad 1 \quad 2$$

$$(1912)$$

STEP 6

When this is done, have your assistant add up the numbers in the answer.
For example:

$$1 + 9 + 1 + 2 = 13$$

STEP 7

When he (she) has added up the numbers, he (she) is to tell you what their sum is (in this case 13). Now, without turning around and looking at the cards, tell your audience that the missing card is the five. This mathematical concept works every time. All you must do to figure out which card is missing, is to take the number he (she) gives you and subtract that number from the number nine. However, if the number he (she) gives you is greater than the number eight, you must subtract the number from 18.

"In order to be truly amazing, you must believe that you are."

Through the Latex

Materials Needed: One quarter, one pill bottle, one piece of latex, one glass, and one rubberband.

Object of Trick: To have the quarter pass through the piece of latex without tearing it.

STEP 1

Prepare this trick by placing the quarter on the top of a small cylinder-shaped item, such as a pill bottle.

STEP 2

Carefully stretch the latex in all four directions until it is so thin it becomes transparent and you can see through it.

STEP 3

Place the latex over the quarter and gently push the quarter up as you release the tension on the latex so the quarter seals itself into the center of the piece of latex. The quarter will look like it is on top of the latex because the latex is so thin it becomes invisible.

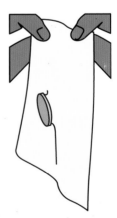

STEP 4

Place the latex over the top of the glass so the quarter is underneath (even though it will appear to be sitting on top of the latex). Next, stretch the rubberband around the top rim of the glass to secure the latex.

STEP 5

Set the glass aside and make certain it does not get moved as the quarter could become dislodged from the latex.

STEP 6

Call in your audience and have them look at the glass. Do not allow any touching!

STEP 7

Ask someone from your audience to be your assistant. Tell him (her) that on the count of three, he (she) is to quickly press on the quarter. The quarter will appear to go through the latex and will land in the bottom of the glass!

Through the Napkin

Materials Needed: One quarter, one cloth napkin, and one marker.

Object of Trick: To have the quarter pass through the napkin without tearing it.

STEP 1
Call in your audience and seat them in front of you, keeping them there at all times. Next, hand someone from your audience the quarter. Have him (her) mark the coin with the marker so he (she) will recognize it again.

STEP 2
Hold the quarter between the thumb and index finger of your left hand in a vertical position.

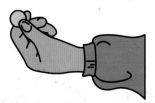

STEP 3
Place the napkin over the quarter so the quarter is in the center of the napkin.

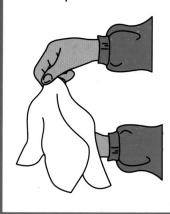

"Looking surprised creates excitement and helps divert your audience's attention."

STEP 4

Carefully, get a small fold of the napkin between your thumb and the quarter. With your right hand, lift the front part of the napkin, facing your audience, and drape it back on top of the other half and over your left wrist.

STEP 5

Show your audience that the quarter is still there.

STEP 6

While still holding the quarter and the napkin, snap your left wrist forward, causing both halves of the napkin to fall forward.

STEP 7

Twist the napkin so it appears that the quarter is wrapped securely in the center of the napkin. Put a little pressure on the edge of the quarter and it will appear to rise up through the napkin!

Pocket Change

Materials Needed: One pocketful of change.

Object of Trick: To trick your audience into thinking you are throwing an actual coin back and forth from one hand to the other.

STEP 1

Pull a handful of change from your pocket and allow your audience to view the coins. Choose one coin and pretend to pick it up — practice doing this by actually picking out a single coin until you can fake it so naturally your audience will have no idea you didn't actually take a coin. Return the change to your pocket.

"Looking at something as if it really exists somehow makes it more realistic."

STEP 2

Throw the imaginary coin back and forth from one hand to the other. You will want to make a small slapping sound coming from the palm of your hand to make your audience think the coin is actually being thrown back and forth. To do this, loosen your fingers and slap them onto the heel of your palm as you catch the fake coin. Practice with a real coin so you can get the sound perfect!

STEP 3

After throwing the imaginary coin back and forth several times, stop the process and pretend to hold the coin in one hand. Ask your audience to choose "heads" or "tails."

STEP 5

Slowly, and very carefully, open your other hand to reveal that the coin isn't there either!

STEP 6

One variation to this trick is to stop the throwing process and pretend to hold the coin in one hand. Instead of asking your audience to choose heads or tails, hold your hand, palm down, and carefully open it. Your audience will be watching for the coin to fall from your hand. When it doesn't, they will assume that the coin is in your other hand. Open it to reveal that the coin isn't there either!

STEP 4

Once the audience chooses heads or tails, slowly open your hand to reveal no coin!

The first reaction from your audience will be to assume that the coin is in your other hand.

The Warm Coin

Materials Needed: Several coins, one hat, a small amount of beeswax (aka magician's wax), and one marker.

Object of Trick: To choose which coin has been marked without looking.

STEP 1
Hand someone from your audience a single coin. Have him (her) mark the coin with the marker so he (she) will recognize it again. While he (she) is marking the coin, place a small amount of beeswax on the tip of your thumbnail.

STEP 2
As you take the coin back from the person in your audience, pretend to take a good look at the coin as you press the wax from your thumbnail onto the edge of the coin.

STEP 3
Drop the coin into the hat and add several more coins. Have a different person from your audience shake the hat to thoroughly mix all of the coins.

STEP 4
Have him (her) hold the hat up. Reach in and feel for the beeswax. Once you find it, remove that coin and quickly scrape the beeswax off. Hand it to the person that marked it for identification!

Ropes
& Rings

"You must
believe in
your magic
in order that
your audience
might also
believe."

Pencil & String

Materials Needed: One 24" length of string, one pencil, and one drill.

Object of Trick: To thread the pencil and string through a buttonhole so it cannot be undone.

STEP 1

Prepare this trick by drilling a hole through the pencil just below the eraser. Next, thread the string through the drilled hole and tie it so when it is pulled tightly, the loop is about one inch from the sharpened end of the pencil.

STEP 2

Call in your audience and seat them in front of you. Next, choose someone from your audience and loop the pencil in one of his (her) buttonholes. Do this by placing the fingers of your right hand through the loop of string.

"Misdirection takes place when you lead your audience's attention away from what is actually happening."

38

STEP 3

Take hold of the buttonhole with your right hand and pull it and the cloth around it through the loop of string. Pull it far enough through the loop so the end of the pencil can be inserted through the buttonhole.

STEP 5

It is now time to have the person remove the pencil from his (her) buttonhole without cutting the string, breaking the pencil, or cutting the buttonhole!

STEP 6

Watch him (her) struggle with this task for as long as your audience is amused — two minutes is usually long enough.

STEP 4

Next, pull the pencil through the buttonhole and pull the looped string tight.

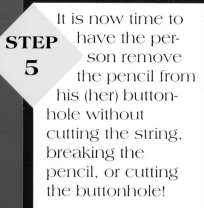

STEP 7

To undo the pencil from the buttonhole, reverse the moves that were used to secure the pencil into the buttonhole as described in steps two and three.

One-Handed Knot

Materials Needed: One 36" length of cotton rope.

Object of Trick: To tie the cotton rope into a knot using only one hand.

STEP 1
Call in your audience and seat them in front of you, keeping them there at all times. Next, drape the cotton rope across your right hand, between your thumb and index finger and behind your pinky.

The end of the rope marked "A" should be longer than "B."

STEP 2
Give an upward jerk to the rope and drop your hand down. Catch the "A" end of the rope between your index and middle fingers.

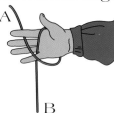

Hold "A" tightly and turn your hand down so the rest of the rope slips off your hand, forming a knot.

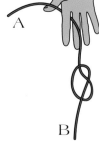

Cut & Restored Rope

Materials Needed: One 48" length of soft cotton rope and one pair of scissors.

Object of Trick: To cut a piece of rope in half and then restore it.

STEP 1

Call in your audience and seat them in front of you, keeping them there at all times. Next, find the middle of the cotton rope and place it over your index finger.

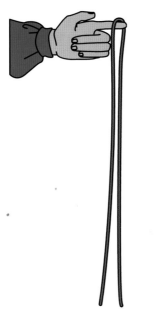

STEP 2

Take one end of the cotton rope, bring it up to the middle, and snugly tie a square knot.

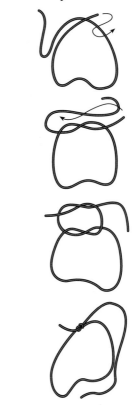

STEP 3

Explain to your audience that the scissors you are going to use are magic scissors. Cut the cotton rope.

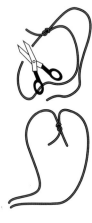

It is absolutely critical that you cut the cotton rope in the correct place!

STEP 4

Once the cut has been made, set the scissors down so that they are out of view. Do this naturally so you do not call attention to where you have placed them.

STEP 5

Hold the cotton rope at each end and pull it tightly so that the rope is displayed with the knot in the center.

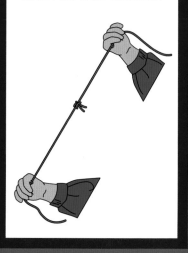

STEP 6

For the grand finale, wrap the cotton rope around one of your hands.

"Having eye contact with your audience is always important."

STEP 7

As you wrap the cotton rope around your hand, the square knot will slide off the cotton rope and must be concealed in your hand.

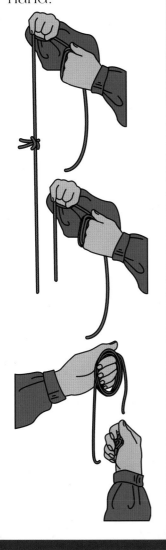

STEP 8

Reach for your magic scissors and quickly discard the small piece of cotton rope.

STEP 9

Wave the magic scissors over your wrapped hand and re-cite some magic words. Set the scissors down once again, this time placing them in view of your audience. Pull the wraps off your hand and hold up the unknotted length of restored cotton rope!

Rope Handcuffs

Materials Needed: Two 24" lengths of cotton rope.

Object of Trick: To tie rope handcuffs on and be able to release them without untying the knots.

STEP 1

Ask for two volunteers from your audience. Tie their wrists together with the cotton ropes exactly as shown and have them try to release themselves without untying the knots.

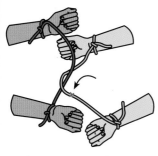

After several minutes of watching them tie themselves into hopeless knots, untie them and ask for another volunteer.

STEP 2

This time you will tie one cotton rope around the wrists of your new volunteer, but make certain you leave a little slack around one of his (her) wrists. Next, ask someone else from your audience to tie your wrists, intertwined with your volunteer's, with the remaining piece of cotton rope. Hopelessly try to wiggle free from each other.

When your hands are out of view of your audience, push the middle of your rope through the loop on your volunteer's wrist and then over his (her) entire hand.

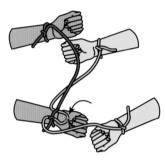

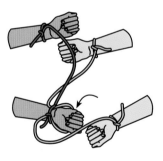

You may have to tell your volunteer to settle down a bit and just relax — this will help you be able to get your rope under his (her) rope.

At this point, you have released the rope that binds the two of you together, but no one knows it yet — not even your volunteer!

Continue to struggle with the ropes. When you are ready to free yourself, all you need to do is pull your wrists toward yourself and you're free!

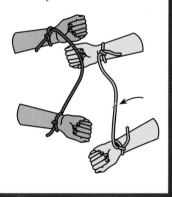

"Learn to
lead your
innocent audience
into an
inescapable trap."

Ring Flip

Materials Needed: One loop of string and one brass ring.

Object of Trick: To catch the brass ring in a knot at the bottom of the loop of string.

STEP 1

Call in your audience and seat them in front of you, keeping them there at all times. Next, hold the loop of string downward, as wide as possible. Place the brass ring about two-thirds of the way up the loop of string and hold the brass ring exactly as shown.

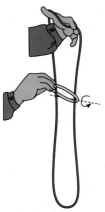

STEP 2

Throw the brass ring down hard toward the bottom of the loop of string. As you throw, flip the brass ring toward the loop of string.

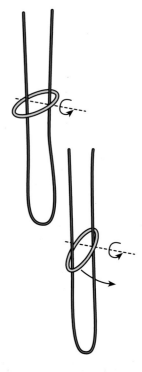

The perfect combination of throw and flip will allow the brass ring to be caught onto the loop of string in a knot at the bottom. Practice makes perfect — at first, expect the brass ring to end up on the floor!

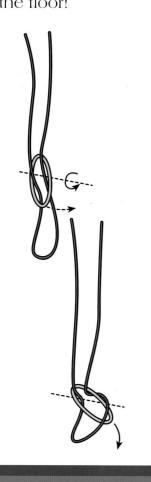

Once the brass ring is secured in the knot at the bottom of the loop of string, hold it up for your audience to view and inspect. They won't believe their eyes!

"The 'secret' is the easiest part of any trick; learning to 'present' the trick will be the hardest."

Locked Ring Release

Materials Needed: One 18" length of string and one brass ring.

Object of Trick: To remove the brass ring from the string without taking it off either end.

STEP 1

Call in your audience and seat them in front of you, keeping them there at all times. Next, place the brass ring on the string and ask someone from your audience to hold one end of the string while you hold the other end. Pull the string taut and place the brass ring in the center of the string.

STEP 2

Grab the brass ring at the bottom and turn it once toward you. Explain to your audience that you are "locking" the brass ring in the string.

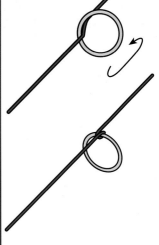

48

Grab the string where it hits the brass ring and let go of your end of the string. Thread your end of the string through the brass ring exactly as shown.

Pull the string taut and explain to your audience that you have now "double locked" the brass ring in the string.

Take hold of the brass ring and give it a spin. When it stops spinning, make certain the string in the center of the brass ring is on the bottom. If it is on the top, simply turn it until it is on the bottom.

Grab the brass ring and move it back and forth on the string as you pull it forward. The locked brass ring will come right off!

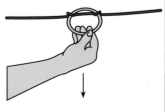

Penetrating Rubberband

Materials Needed: One rubberband and one men's ring.

Object of Trick: To make the rubberband pass through the men's ring.

STEP 1

Call in your audience and seat them in front of you, keeping them there at all times. Next, pass the rubberband and the men's ring around so your audience can carefully inspect each one.

STEP 3

If you have pinched the rubberband inside the ring correctly, you should be able to move the ring up and down by stretching the rubberband. However, it should appear that the rubberband has penetrated the ring!

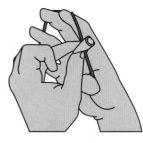

STEP 2

Hold the rubberband and the ring as shown.

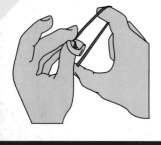

Mental Magic

"Magic
could
possibly be
the most
ancient of
all the
human arts."

Color Cards

Materials Needed: Six index cards and one black marker.

Object of Trick: To choose the correct color.

STEP 1

Prepare this trick by writing the name of a different color on each index card. Make certain each word has a different number of letters: red (3), pink (4), white (5), purple (6), fuschia (7), and lavender (8).

STEP 2

Call in your audience and seat them. Place the six index cards in random order on the table with the color words facing up.

LAVENDER	PURPLE
RED	PINK
WHITE	FUSCHIA

STEP 3

Ask someone from your audience to pick a color. He (she) must not tell anyone the name of the color. Next, ask him (her) to silently spell the name of the color, one letter at a time, as you touch each card. When he (she) reaches the last letter of the color word, tell him (her) to say, "Stop!" For the first two letters, touch any card. Beginning with the third letter, you *must* touch the three-letter card. Next, touch the four-letter card and so on. When you hear "Stop!" — you will be on the correct color card.

Clever Codes

Materials Needed: One blindfolded assistant.

Object of Trick: To choose the correct objects from around the room.

STEP 1

Ask someone from your audience to blindfold your assistant. Next, stand your assistant in a corner of the room, facing the wall.

STEP 2

The person whom you chose from your audience must now walk around the room and touch any object — such as a lantern. Next, ask your assistant, "Did he (she) touch the floor? The coffee table? The mantle? The lantern?" Excitedly, your assistant says, "Yes, he (she) touched the lantern!"

STEP 3

Continue until your assistant has identified several more objects that members of your audience have touched. Do not alter the tone of your voice as you talk to your assistant. A pre-arranged verbal code should be practiced. For example, the object touched will be the first one you mention after you name an object that begins with the letter M (mantle). Use a word as your "key" letters — such as MAGIC. Each time you do the trick, use the next letter.

Master Memory

Materials Needed: One blackboard, one piece of chalk, and one blindfold.

Object of Trick: To memorize a list of 10 objects.

STEP 1

Prepare this trick by making up a list of 10 objects and memorizing them. Use the following objects to practice:

1. Apple

2. Birdhouse

3. Radio

4. Guitar

5. Car

6. Fork

7. Television

8. Fish

9. Necklace

10. Snake

STEP 2

Call in your audience and seat them. Ask someone from your audience to blindfold you and stand you with your back to the blackboard. Next, have the audience list 10 objects, one at a time.

STEP 3

The person whom you chose from your audience must write these objects down on the blackboard, and number them from one to 10. You will now name the object that matches the corresponding number.

STEP 4

Once you have memorized your list of 10 objects, you need to create mental images connecting the objects that the audience has chosen with those in your own list. The sillier the mental images the better — they will help you remember easier. Let's say the audience's list has the following objects:

1.   Ball

2.   Pencil

3.   Nickel

4.   Jar

5.   Cow

6.   Eraser

7.   Paper Clip

8.   Rock

9.   Yo-Yo

10. Dice

STEP 5

Create a mental image of the two objects in the number one positions: the apple and the ball. Imagine the apple being used as a ball in a baseball game.

For the next one, create a mental image of the objects in the number two positions: the birdhouse and the pencil. How about the birdhouse with a pencil as the perch?

Clever Clock

Materials Needed: One photocopy of the face of a clock and one pencil.

Object of Trick: To choose the correct number.

STEP 1 Show someone from your audience the photocopy of the clock's face. Have him (her) mentally select one of the numbers and then have him (her) add one to the number. Make certain he (she) remembers the number, because he (she) will begin counting at that number, when you begin tapping your pencil on the clock's face.

"For a split second, you want time to stand still."

STEP 2 Have him (her) continue counting silently each time you tap your pencil. When he (she) gets to 20 he (she) is to say, "Stop!"

STEP 3 Use your pencil to circle the correct number on the clock's face. Next, hand him (her) the paper, face down, and have him (her) tell your audience what number he (she) originally chose — the number before he (she) added one. At this time, have him (her) turn the paper over to reveal your answer!

Amazingly, your answer will be correct every time. The trick is to always begin tapping your pencil at number six. Proceed *counter clockwise* around the clock's face. When your helper from the audience reaches 20 and says, "Stop!," you will be on the correct number. This trick can be repeated as many times as you'd like to do it, but make certain no one sees where you begin tapping each time!

PATTERN

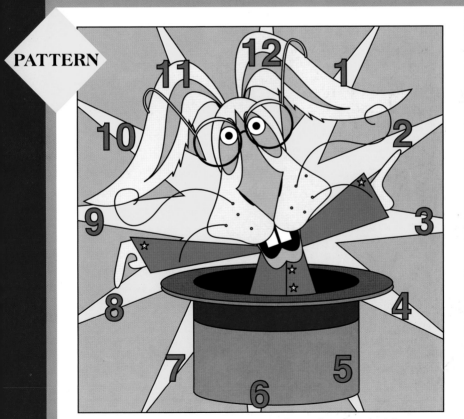

Use this pattern to make photocopies!

Subtraction & Addition

Materials Needed: One piece of paper and one pencil.

Object of Trick: To choose the correct number.

STEP 1

Ask someone from your audience to write any five-digit number on the piece of paper. This number is to be made up of five different numbers — he (she) must not use the same number twice. For example:

4 7 9 5 2

STEP 2

Next, have him (her) reverse the order of the numbers, then write them down underneath the first set of numbers and subtract them.

```
  4 7 9 5 2
− 2 5 9 7 4
─────────
  2 1 9 7 8
```

STEP 3

Have him (her) write this number down, in reverse order, underneath it and add them.

```
  2 1 9 7 8
+ 8 7 9 1 2
─────────
1 0 9,8 9 0
```

STEP 4

It is now time for him (her) to concentrate on that number and you are going to read his (her) mind. The answer will almost always be 109,890, but occasionally it will be 99,099. If you are wrong, pretend you have picked up someone else's vibes and ask for one more chance!

Famous Names

Materials Needed: Ten 2" x 3" cards, one piece of paper, one pencil, and one hat.

Object of Trick: To choose the correct name.

STEP 1

Ask someone from your audience to call out the names of ten different famous people as you write them down on the cards. Let's say the first name is Queen Elizabeth. Write "Queen Elizabeth" on the first card. Let's say the second name is Napoleon. Write "Queen Elizabeth" on the second card, and so on, until all ten cards have "Queen Elizabeth" written on them. You must do this so your audience thinks you are writing the names being given.

STEP 2

As you write the name on each card, put it into the hat. This assures that your audience will not be able to see what you are actually writing on the cards.

STEP 3

Ask another volunteer from your audience to mix the cards in the hat and pick one out. Have him (her) concentrate on the name. After a few seconds tell your audience you believe you have read his (her) mind and recite to the audience the name of the person!

59

Phone Book Phenomenon

Materials Needed: One piece of paper, one pencil, and one phone book.

Object of Trick: To choose the correct name of the person in the phone book.

STEP 1

Prepare this trick by looking in the phone book on page 108. Count down nine lines and memorize the name(s) of the person(s) listed in that space.

STEP 2

Ask someone from your audience to call out three different numbers as you write them down on the paper. Show the paper to your audience so they know you have written down the numbers, exactly as they were given to you.

STEP 3

Ask another volunteer from your audience to come up to assist you. Let's say you have already written on the paper the numbers:

9 3 1

Have him (her) write this number down, in reverse order, underneath it and subtract them.

$$
\begin{array}{r}
9\ 3\ 1 \\
-\ 1\ 3\ 9 \\
\hline
7\ 9\ 2
\end{array}
$$

60

STEP 4

Next, have the volunteer from your audience reverse those numbers, then add the two numbers together.

$$
\begin{array}{r}
7\,9\,2 \\
+\ 2\,9\,7 \\
\hline
1\,0\,8\,9
\end{array}
$$

STEP 5

No matter what combination of numbers are used, the answer will always be 1089. However, if only two numbers result from the subtraction problem, simply add a zero at the left. For example, if the difference of the subtraction problem were 32, it would become 032.

STEP 6

Next, have the person from your audience that gave you the original numbers look into the phone book and go to the page number that is indicated by the first three numbers from your mathematical equation, in this case (and every case!) page 108. When he (she) has turned to page 108, have him (her) count down to the listing indicated by the fourth number from your equation, in this case the ninth listing. Have him (her) concentrate on the name(s). After a few seconds, tell your audience you believe you have read his (her) mind and recite the name(s) of the person(s)!

Mathematical Mystery

Materials Needed: One piece of paper and one pencil.

Object of Trick: To choose the correct answer.

STEP 1

Ask someone from your audience to call out a single digit number as you write it down on the piece of paper. Show the paper to your audience.

STEP 2

Now take that number and double it. Next, add four, then divide by two. Finally, subtract the original number. Let's say the number is: 2. Double it to get 4. Add 4 to get 8. Divide by 2 to get 4. Subtract 2. Your answer is 2.

STEP 3

Your answer will always be one-half of the number you add. For example, if you add 4 (as in this case), your answer will be 2. If you add 10, your answer will be 5. Let's say the number is: 2. Double it to get 4. Add 10 to get 14. Divide by 2 to get 7. Subtract 2 to get your answer — which is 5 — one-half of the number you added!

STEP 4

Use a different adding number each time to get a different answer.

You're Right, They Match!

Materials Needed: Two pieces of paper and two pencils.

Object of Trick: To write the same sentence.

STEP 1

Ask someone from your audience to write a sentence on one of the pieces of paper. Next, have him (her) fold it and hand it to another person in your audience.

STEP 2

Take the other piece of paper and tell your audience you are going to write the same sentence. You will then write, "You're right, they match!" on your piece of paper. Fold it and hand it to the same person who is holding the matching sentence.

STEP 3

Ask your volunteer to open the paper containing the sentence written by the person from your audience and to read it out loud.

STEP 4

Now, ask your volunteer to open the paper containing the sentence you wrote and to read it out loud. He will laugh and say, "You're right, they match!" Your audience will be amazed — at least until your volunteer spills the beans!

Fruits & Vegetables

Materials Needed: One piece of paper, three pencils, and one hat.

Object of Trick: To choose the piece of paper with the name of the vegetable written on it.

STEP 1

Prepare this trick by tearing a sheet of notebook paper into three equal pieces. Do not cut the paper; you will need to have the "torn" edges to aid you in performing this trick.

STEP 2

Call in your audience and seat them. Ask for three volunteers to assist you. Have two volunteers write the name of a fruit on their pieces of paper. Have one volunteer write the name of a vegetable on his (her) piece of paper.

STEP 3

It is critical that you hand the "middle" piece of paper to the volunteer that is to write the name of a vegetable on his (her) piece of paper. This piece will have two torn sides which will identify it from the other two pieces of paper.

STEP 4

Have another volunteer from your audience place the papers into the hat and mix them up. Reach into the hat and pull out the paper with the name of the vegetable!

Outrageous Others

"Magic
tricks
should
never be
repeated
before the
same audience."

French Drop

Materials Needed: One half-dollar.

Object of Trick: To make the half-dollar disappear.

STEP 1

Call in your audience and seat them in front of you, keeping them there at all times. Next, hold the half-dollar as shown.

STEP 2

Turn your hand so your audience can see both sides of the half-dollar.

STEP 3

Move both hands toward one another, moving the hand holding the half-dollar more.

Front View

Back View

"Magic is making the impossible possible."

STEP 4

Drop the half-dollar onto your "ring" finger and pinch it as shown. This is known as the finger palm.

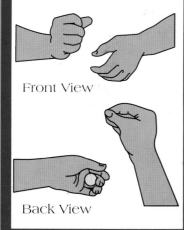

Front View

Back View

STEP 6

Bring your empty hand into full view. Your audience thinks the coin is in it. Look at it and move it around.

STEP 7

Tell your audience that the half dollar is now inside someone's ear. Choose someone from your audience and reach out with the empty hand to retrieve the half-dollar from their ear. When you come up empty, look surprised. Then, reach out with the other hand to retrieve the half-dollar from their other ear and, of course, there you'll find it!

STEP 5

Once you have the half-dollar in your finger palm, allow your arm to fall to your side. Make certain you keep your fingers relaxed.

Paper Clip Union

Materials Needed: One dollar bill and two paper clips.

Object of Trick: To make the paper clips unite.

STEP 1

Call in your audience and seat them in front of you, keeping them there at all times. Next, fold the dollar bill into a "Z-shape."

STEP 3

Hold up the dollar bill so your audience can take a good look at it. Warn the members of your audience sitting on the front row to beware!

STEP 2

Place the paper clips on the dollar bill exactly as shown.

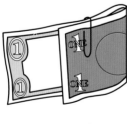

STEP 4

Hold the dollar bill at each end and quickly snap it into a straightened position. The paper clips will link themselves together and fly up and out, possibly into the audience!

Paper Clip Union Enhanced

Materials Needed: One dollar bill and four paper clips.

Object of Trick: To make the paper clips unite.

STEP 1

Call in your audience and seat them in front of you, keeping them there at all times. Next, link two paper clips together until you have two paper clip chains as shown.

STEP 3

Hold up the dollar bill so your audience can take a good look at it.

STEP 4

Hold the dollar bill at each end and quickly snap it into a straightened position. The paper clip chains will link themselves together and fly up and out.

STEP 2

Fold the dollar bill into a "Z-shape" and place the paper clip chains on the dollar bill as shown on page 68.

Paper Money Flip-Flop

Materials Needed: One dollar bill.

Object of Trick: To turn the dollar bill upside down by folding it twice and then unfolding it.

STEP 1
Hold the dollar bill upright by holding it at each side.

STEP 2
Next, fold the dollar bill in half length-wise and make a crease along the fold.

STEP 3
Next, fold the dollar bill in half exactly as shown and make a crease along the fold.

STEP 4
Carefully unfold the dollar bill beginning at the bottom left hand corner to reveal that it is now upside down!

Broken Toothpick

Materials Needed: Two toothpicks and one handkerchief.

Object of Trick: To restore a broken toothpick.

STEP 1
Prepare this trick by placing a toothpick into the hem of a handkerchief and pushing it to the middle.

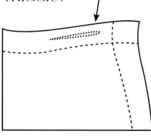

STEP 2
Call in your audience and seat them in front of you. Next, show your audience the remaining toothpick and place it in the center of the handkerchief.

STEP 3
Wrap it up by folding the corner of the handkerchief up under its center. Ask someone from your audience to break the toothpick in two. He (she) will feel the toothpick in the hem and as it breaks, your audience will be able to hear it snap. Make certain the toothpick that you placed in the center of the handkerchief does not fall out.

STEP 4
Unwrap the toothpick from the handkerchief to prove your point!

71

Spinning Egg

Materials Needed: Eleven fresh eggs and one hard-boiled egg.

Object of Trick: To spin an egg.

STEP 1
Prepare this trick by hard-boiling one of the eggs.

STEP 2
When the egg has cooled, place it back in the egg carton with the fresh eggs in a position you will remember.

STEP 3
Call in your audience and seat them in front of you. Next, pass out eggs to eleven of them, taking the hard-boiled one for yourself.

STEP 4
Using your egg, which no one knows is hard-boiled, demonstrate how you would like them to spin their eggs. One at a time, have each person come up to the table and attempt to spin his (her) egg. No one will be able to do it because fresh, raw eggs will not spin.

STEP 5
You may choose to have two of the eggs hard-boiled. That way one of your volunteers will be able to spin his (her) egg and you can make a big deal out of it!

Balancing Egg

Materials Needed: One dozen fresh eggs and some table salt.

Object of Trick: To balance an egg.

STEP 1 Prepare this trick by shaking one of the eggs so the yolk settles. After shaking the egg, the trick must be performed relatively soon or the egg will need to be shaken again.

STEP 2 Place the egg back in the egg carton in a position you will remember.

STEP 3 Call in your audience and seat them in front of you. Next, pass out eggs to eleven of them, taking the shaken one for yourself.

STEP 4 Using your egg, which no one knows has been shaken, demonstrate how you would like for them to stand their eggs on their large ends. One at a time, have each person come up to the table and attempt to balance his (her) egg. No one will be able to do it.

STEP 5 If necessary, put some table salt in a little mound on the table. Press your egg into the table salt and it will help to balance the egg. Do this so no ones knows the salt is present!

73

Egg Drop Soup

Materials Needed: Three eggs, three empty toilet paper rolls, one broom, one pie plate, and three wide-mouth glasses half-full of water.

Object of Trick: To have the eggs end up in the half-full glasses of water.

STEP 1

Prepare this trick by choosing an ideal location outdoors for your performance. The edge of a picnic table works well, but make certain the picnic table has been completely cleared off.

STEP 2

Call for your audience and have them stand around, but away from, the picnic table.

STEP 3

Set up your trick on the edge of the picnic table exactly as shown. Make certain that the eggs you are using are large enough to "perch" on the top of the toilet paper rolls. If they are too small, they might fall into the roll. If they are too large, they might become wedged in the roll.

Double check to make certain that you have the pie plate hanging over the edge of the picnic table.

Place the broom in front of you as you face the table. The bristles of the broom should be directly below the pie plate.

Step on the bristles of the broom and grab ahold of the broom handle. Pull it back toward you. As you let go, the broom handle should hit the pie plate straight on.

Things will fly, but unbelievably the three eggs will be inside the half-full glasses of water — a magician's recipe for egg drop soup!

Find the Rattle

Materials Needed: Four small matchboxes, two dimes, and one rubberband.

Object of Trick: To choose the matchbox containing the dime.

STEP 1

Prepare this trick by placing a dime into one of the small matchboxes. Secure it to your left wrist with a wide rubberband. Make certain it is under your sleeve and hidden from the view of your audience.

STEP 2

Call in your audience and seat them in front of you. Next, place the remaining three matchboxes on the table and show your audience that they are empty.

STEP 3

Take the remaining dime and and place it into one of the matchboxes. As you close the box, let the dime slip out of the box and into your hand where you will conceal it from your audience.

STEP 4

Close the last two matchboxes and rotate them to mix them all up. Pick up one of the matchboxes with your left hand and shake it. It will sound as though the dime is inside.

STEP 5
Have your audience keep a close eye on this matchbox. Once again, mix them all up.

STEP 8
Ask someone else from your audience to pick up one of the remaining matchboxes and shake it. It will not rattle.

STEP 6
Ask someone from your audience to choose which matchbox he (she) feels is the matchbox containing the dime. Have him (her) pick it up and shake it. It will be empty.

STEP 9
With your right hand, pick up the last matchbox and open it. As you pick it up, let the dime that you have concealed in your palm drop onto the table. It should appear that it fell from inside the opened matchbox.

STEP 7
Repeat these steps several times. Then ask someone from your audience to pick up one of the matchboxes and shake it. It will not rattle.

"Revealing any secrets to your audience turns even the best magic into nothing more than cheap tricks."

Invisible Ball

Materials Needed: One clear sandwich bag.

Object of Trick: To catch the invisible ball in the sandwich bag.

STEP 1

Show your audience the sandwich bag. Because it is clear, your audience will be able to see through the sandwich bag, but will not be able to see the invisible ball inside.

STEP 2

Explain that you are going to throw the invisible ball up into the air and that you will attempt to catch it in the sandwich bag.

STEP 3

Reach into the sandwich bag and pull out the invisible ball. Next, throw the imaginary ball into the air. As you do this, you must quickly raise the sandwich bag as though you are attempting to catch the ball. These two actions must be performed at the same time. As you raise the sandwich bag, snap your fingers. If the sandwich bag is in between your finger and your thumb when you "snap," it will sound like the ball is falling into the sandwich bag!

Conversion Charts

INCHES TO MILLIMETRES AND CENTIMETRES
MM-Millimetres   CM-Centimetres

INCHES	MM	CM	INCHES	CM	INCHES	CM
1/8	3	0.9	9	22.9	30	76.2
1/4	6	0.6	10	25.4	31	78.7
3/8	10	1.0	11	27.9	32	81.3
1/2	13	1.3	12	30.5	33	83.8
5/8	16	1.6	13	33.0	34	86.4
3/4	19	1.9	14	35.6	35	88.9
7/8	22	2.2	15	38.1	36	91.4
1	25	2.5	16	40.6	37	94.0
1 1/4	32	3.2	17	43.2	38	96.5
1 1/2	38	3.8	18	45.7	39	99.1
1 3/4	44	4.4	19	48.3	40	101.6
2	51	5.1	20	50.8	41	104.1
2 1/2	64	6.4	21	53.3	42	106.7
3	76	7.6	22	55.9	43	109.2
3 1/2	89	8.9	23	58.4	44	111.8
4	102	10.2	24	61.0	45	114.3
4 1/2	114	11.4	25	63.5	46	116.8
5	127	12.7	26	66.0	47	119.4
6	152	15.2	27	68.6	48	121.9
7	178	17.8	28	71.1	49	124.5
8	203	20.3	29	73.7	50	127.0

If the coins that have been used in these tricks are not available, coins of approximate size will work.

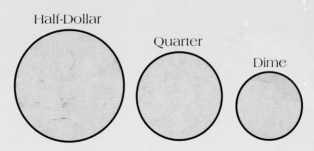

Half-Dollar

Quarter

Dime

Index